A Little
Daylight Left

A Little
Daylight Left

SARAH KAY

THE DIAL PRESS
NEW YORK

Published in the United States by The Dial Press, an imprint of Random House, a division of Penguin Random House LLC, New York.

THE DIAL PRESS is a registered trademark and the colophon is a trademark of Penguin Random House LLC.

Library of Congress Cataloging-in-Publication Data
Names: Kay, Sarah, 1988- author.
Title: A little daylight left / Sarah Kay.
Description: New York: The Dial Press, 2025. |
Identifiers: LCCN 2024046238 (print) | LCCN 2024046239 (ebook) |
ISBN 9780593733707 (hardcover) | ISBN 9780593733714 (ebook)
Subjects: LCGFT: Poetry.
Classification: LCC PS3611.A887 L58 2025 (print) | LCC PS3611.A887 (ebook) |
DDC 811/.6—dc23/eng/20241004
LC record available at https://lccn.loc.gov/2024046238
LC ebook record available at https://lccn.loc.gov/2024046239

Printed in Canada on acid-free paper

randomhousebooks.com

9 8 7 6 5 4 3 2 1

FIRST EDITION

For the moment when the streetlights come on
& for my folks

A BIRD MADE OF BIRDS

"The universe has already written the poem you were planning on writing"
—Kaveh Akbar

The universe has already written the poem you were planning on writing
& this is why   you can do nothing   but point
at the flock of starlings   whose bodies rise & fall
in inherited choreography   swarming the sky in a sweeping curtain
that for one blistering moment   forms the unmistakable shape
of a giant bird flapping against the sky.   It is why your mouth
forms an   *Oh*   that is not a gasp   but rather the beginning of
Oh of course   as in—   of course the heart of a blue whale
is as large as a house   with chambers tall enough to fit a person standing.
Of course   a fig becomes possible   when a lady wasp
lays her eggs inside a flower   dies   & decomposes
the fruit—evidence of her transformation.   Sometimes
the poem is so bright   your silly language will not stick to it.
Sometimes the poem is so true   nobody will believe you.
I am a bird   made of birds   this blue heart a house
you can stand up inside of.   I am dying   here   inside this flower.
It is ok.   It is what I was put here to do.   Take this fruit.
It is what I have to offer.   It may not be first   or ever best
but it is the only way to be sure   I lived at all.

CONTENTS

III

A Little
Daylight Left

there are enough ballrooms in you to dance with everyone you'll ever love
—Laura Lamb Brown-Lavoie

& remember / loneliness is still time spent / with the world
—Ocean Vuong

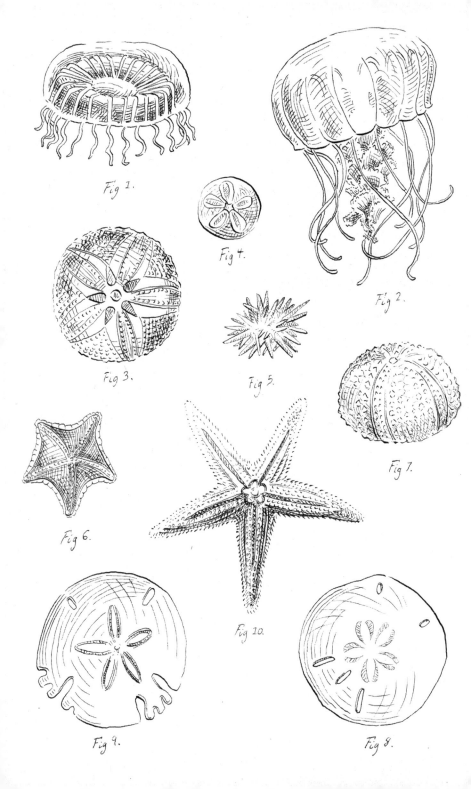

Fig 1.

Fig 4.

Fig 2.

Fig 3.

Fig 5.

Fig 7.

Fig 6.

Fig 10.

Fig 9.

Fig 8.

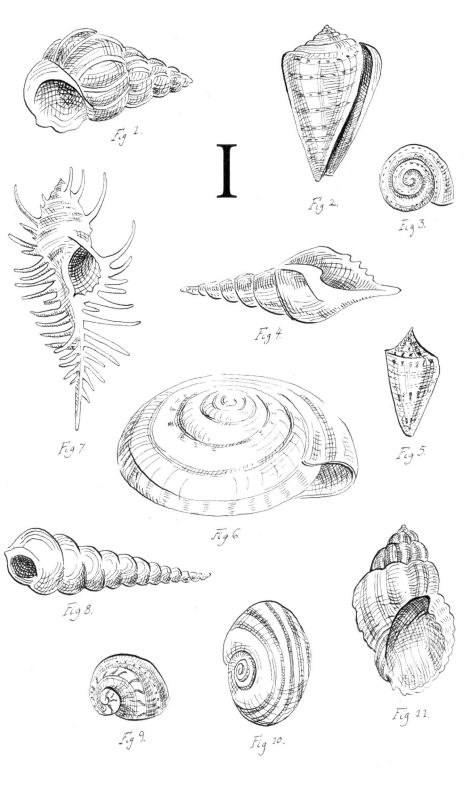

Fig 1.

I

Fig 2.

Fig 3.

Fig 4.

Fig 7.

Fig 5.

Fig 6.

Fig 8.

Fig 9.

Fig 10.

Fig 11.

ODE TO THE TWO GIRLS IN THE OUTFIELD OF THE TEE BALL GAME

Somewhere nearby a ball
is hurtling through the air
or tumbling towards the pitcher's mound,
an orchestra of parents erupting into the spring breeze,
but we don't know anything about that.
We have forgotten the game entirely,
have forgotten that technically,
somebody is supposed
to be *left field* & someone *right,*
that we were given instructions
about looking skyward,
& keeping our gloves poised & ready—
we have forgotten the gloves. Have abandoned them,
our fingers interlaced or braiding blades of grass,
there is no left or right here. Just field.
Just butterflies & bees, the soft hum one of us offers
of a song we might or might not know.
One of us has a tooth we can wiggle.
One of us puts on our glove as a hat.
We are making wishes on eyelashes & pinky promises.
Somewhere there are girls who keep their eye on the ball.
Somewhere boys who grab for a wrist
when a girl rounds the base for home.
Out here there are only dandelions.
I am wearing the same jersey as you
but mine has a different number
& yours is backwards,
& that is enough to make us laugh.
We laugh & laugh & laugh
& a planet blooms in our laughter.
Our planet is open for business.
Business is trading sunshine for freckles
& business is booming.
The sky is laughing.
The sky has forgotten the game entirely.

Somewhere somebody is winning & somebody is losing
& they are wearing the same jerseys as we are but
they have forgotten the point entirely.
Soon
someone will call our names
someone will summon us back to earth
someone will grab our wrists & remind us of the rules
but not yet.
Not before we have named every cloud,
compared every freckle,
serenaded every bee.
Teach me how to cartwheel like you.
Press your body into the grass beside me,
I want to be able to see where we once were.

RACCOON

I am too young & too New York City
to know
that this is a raccoon
staring back at me
through the sliding glass door of my uncle's cabin.
It could just as easily be a cat
who has not gotten enough sleep lately,
or a cat who got popped one in the nose
& earned himself two shiners,
which might be what he earns again
if he keeps digging through the trash cans on the porch.

I am too young & too alone in the den
to know not to slide open the glass door for a closer look,
while the grown-ups are cleaning up dinner in the kitchen
& the cousins are shooting at ducks on the TV screen
with plastic orange guns that they do not share with me.

I am too young & too small
to scare him, so he does not run,
just holds tight the scrap of fish skin he has found.
& I know that cats like fish!
But I have never seen a cat stand on his hind legs before.
So maybe this is a Magic Cat.

I am young enough to know
that when you meet a Magic Cat
you must bring him a gift,
& so even though he already has some fish,
I raise my plate,
which I was taking to the grown-ups in the kitchen,
but now serve with both hands as an offering.

The Magic Cat hops down from the railing
& now we are face to face.
& now two more tiny Magic Cats

appear from out of the dark!
& they are all sharing my gift together!

& for a moment, I am a sorceress.
Because after the Magic Cats come the Magic Fairies, I know.
& the dragons & wolves,
the ninjas & spies, the adventures & quests.
For a moment everything is possible
& here,
& licking at my plate,
& I am lost in the blackest eyes & softest fur.

& then everyone is screaming behind me!

& the cats disappear
& the plate is taken from my hands
& the trash is double-bagged
& the lids are weighed down with rocks
& the glass door is locked
& the uncles are shaking their heads
& the cousins are laughing
& the aunties are trying to explain the difference
between a pet & a wild animal
& I am so young & so embarrassed
& so painfully unmagic.

& later,
when I am old enough to know the animals you can keep
from the ones you cannot,
when I am old enough to know
a cat from a raccoon,
a sorceress from a lonely girl,
magic from survival,
later,
when you knock on my glass door
& come in from out of the dark night,
is it any wonder
that for one entire holy moment,
I am sure
that I have seen you somewhere before?

RARE

There was a tarantula in the terrarium
that hung above the pool table in the greenroom
of the rock club in the Meatpacking District
that my babysitter Parker took me to one afternoon
to see her boyfriend Tim practice with his band.
& when people ask if growing up in New York City
was full of rare experiences I always shrug
& fail to think of even one, because it is impossible
to know what is rare when you have no comparison.
I had no comparison because Tim was the first boyfriend
I had ever met, though I did know he was broad as a doorway,
with forearms like tree branches & a look that made Parker blush
on nights when he came to pick her up, which I watched
from my bedroom's secret darkness: her lightbulb face
set aglow by his voice's low rumble,
his eyes two moths for her alone.
Parker, with her southern accent & threadbare t-shirts,
who spent all afternoon making me PB&Js
while she sang along to Hard Day's Night,
tossing the bangs of the dark pixie mullet she cut herself,
sometimes in our bathroom sink,
who always came straight from dance rehearsal
& needed to stretch her hamstrings,
pausing to sniff her armpits as she pulled her forehead to her knees,
face twisting in disgust & pride,
woman, adored—I understood,
from the way the air between them hummed,
the oozy laughter they erupted in each other,
the way she never dimmed in his presence:
still my Parker, smelly & strong, acned & calloused,
silly, confident, luminous, megawatt.
When we heard the music start,
we left the greenroom & the tarantula
& headed down to be an audience of two
for the mid-day rehearsal,
the empty rock club dance floor ours alone,
from which we could perfectly

make out the bright pearls around Tim's neck
bouncing against his lumberjack chest above his tank top,
his skirt flouncing about his knees
as he stomped out the rhythm,
& it would take me years to visit the suburbs for the first time
& look around thinking, *wow, just like in the movies,*
everything alien & clean: bike rides to the end of a cul de sac
& a neighbor waving from a driveway,
a cheer squad & a boy in a varsity jacket,
& it would take me so many more years
to learn that what I saw in the bar *was* rare:
not the man in the pearls & the skirt,
not his girlfriend sweaty beneath the strobe lights, no,
what was rare was the electric joy made possible
when you do not only watch but also see each other,
when you are not only performing but also practicing,
your onliest edges unhidden, offered to a lover's open palms.

ARS POETICA

Thirteen already & therefore behind
on my bat mitzvah training
I sit in the office of the Rabbi for our first meeting
so ready to be the best student
to show my work & get my head pats
my gold stars
of David or whatever
there is to be earned
instead she slides me
the first fountain pen
I have ever held
& tells me it is mine
I like the way the ink escapes
but also its freedom
makes me nervous
just like she does
when she asks how I plan to relate
my torah portion to
everything that's happened

I know you live downtown   she says
is your family back in your home yet
I light up at the chance
to share our proximity to *Ground Zero*
as though proximity might make it mine
instead she says
You know only Rabbis are allowed
to handle certain bodies
I went down because they said
they needed help handling   identifying but
there were barely any
                        bodies
the dust   the ash
                        I've never
at last   a hand
                        at least

there was a hand
we knew who it belonged to
I carried it in a bucket
made a body bag look full
tucked it into the zipper
so the family might believe
the rest of him was there
by the time she returns to the office
I am the curtains
    a part of the chair
that night my mother is furious
that she would tell this story to *a child*
& for twenty years I do not write it down

because I only know
how to write love letters
& send them into space
because I only know
how to write what is mine
& what of any of that was mine?
not the story
    not the hand
        not the Rabbi
        not the bucket
     not the City
not the ash
    or the dust or my mother's anger
        not even the fountain pen
       though I did keep that
     & still went back for my next meeting & practiced
until I could say the prayers without looking
& I still can't tell you what any of the words mean
but I can tell you that when I stand next to my father & say them
he hears his own father's voice
so I know I will hear his
when he isn't singing next to me any longer
& maybe that is what is mine—
    this search for mercy
       what it weighs
       & the place I make to set it down

JAKARTA, JANUARY

After Hanif Abdurraqib & Frank O'Hara

It is the last class of the day &
I am teaching a classroom of sixth graders about poetry
& across town a man walks into a Starbucks & blows himself up
while other men throw grenades in the street & shoot
into the crowd of civilians & I am twenty-seven years old
which means I am the only person in this room who was alive
when this happened in New York City & I was in eighth grade
& sitting in my classroom for the first class of the day
& I made a joke about how mad everyone was going to be
at the pilot who messed up & then later added
how stupid do you have to be for it to happen twice?
& the sixth graders are practicing listing sensory details
& somebody calls out *blue skies* as a sight they love
& nobody in this classroom knows what has happened yet
& they do not know that the school is in *lockdown*
which is a word we did not have when I was their age
& the whole class is laughing because a boy has called out *dog poop*
as a smell he does not like & what is a boy
if not a glowing thing learning what he can get away with
& I was once a girl in a classroom on the lucky side of town
who did not know what had happened yet
& *electrical fire* is a smell I did not know I did not like
until my neighborhood smelled that way for weeks
& *blue skies* is a sight I have never trusted again
& poetry is what I reached for
in the days when the ash would not stop falling
& there is a sixth grade girl in this classroom
whose father is inside that Starbucks & she does not know
what has happened yet & what is a girl
if not a pulsing thing learning what the world will take from her
& what if I am still a girl sitting in my classroom
on the lucky side of town making a careless joke
looking up at my teacher for some sort of answer
& what if I am also the teacher without any answers
looking back at myself & what is an adult

if not a terrified thing desperate to protect something you cannot save
& how lucky do you have to be for it to miss you twice?
& tomorrow a sixth grade girl will come to class
while her father has the shrapnel pulled from his body
& maybe she will reach for poetry & the sky
outside the classroom is so terribly blue
& the students are quiet & looking at me
& waiting for a poem or an answer
or a grown-up or a bell to ring
& the bell rings & they float up
out of their seats like tiny ghosts & are gone.

ACROSS THE ROOM

everyone is talking over each other
the familiar music of women
of a certain age
behind closed doors
the wind chime laughter
& comfort
of formless ankle-length dresses
& a couch full of mothers
who are not my mother
other than the one who is
my mother
who is chatting
about Old New York
her truest love her longest partner
whose arms she ran into
to escape
the relentless sunshine of California
I grin to hear her
talk about this city the way
I have always heard her talk
about this city the way
I have never heard her talk
about anyone or anything else
the adoration of a younger woman
still bubbling through her
the quiet bell of her voice
arriving only in snippets
across the room
someone asks
if we need more tea &   *the elevator door of the office building opened*
                            there they were   one held a gun to my head

someone asks
if the L train is running
& someone jokes about being
the oldest woman on the L train
laughter clangs through
the living room   *forced me to the bathroom   pulled down my pants*

I cannot read her lips
clearly enough
the tea
is brewed
so we pour   *lucky, really*
someone's son
is back from college
someone is asking
about redoing
their kitchen   *If his buddy hadn't come in just then*
                              but he said   what are you doing   we have to go

a woman taps
my shoulder &
asks me how
the Poetry is going   *anyway I've always loved downtown more*
                              my mother shrugs   & sips her tea

It is going
I manage to answer
I am sure you must have
so many stories to share
the woman says
Your father is such
an excellent storyteller
always commands a room
is that where you get it from
I wonder

THE MESSAGE

On the grey & sullen Washington beach
the tide went out so far each day
I could walk a half mile before reaching the water
the damp sand unveiling its misshapen leftovers from the night before
& most days I wasn't out there alone
usually a bald eagle or someone fetching mussels from a crate
& one day I noticed a boy
I mean he couldn't have been more than ten
collecting sand dollars in a bucket
& then stacking them in his hands once the bucket was full
& I felt compelled
I mean it felt like it was only us out there
& so I felt I must
I mean I reached him & told him
I mean I showed him how to tell
if a sand dollar was dead
the peekabooing bone hue
slumped beneath some seaweed or
deep in tide pool murk
then I showed him how to spot the live ones
grey or black even brown sometimes growing a soft green fur
far uglier in their living than their death & so
I hoped he would leave them alone
I mean I wanted to believe that I had taught him
to collect only what was not tethered to the earth
I mean I didn't know if a sand dollar had a soul but
I didn't want a massacre on my hands
I mean his hands
I mean I walked away
hoping he had gotten the message
don't just take because you can

but now I can feel
the man's hands
that reached through the gap between airplane seats
to grope me out of slumber
my shock at what could still find me

even thousands of miles in the air
only he wasn't a man   he was a boy
I mean he couldn't have been more than fourteen
half my age I mean
he could have been one of my students I mean
my impulse was to teach him
I mean I couldn't stop thinking
it was my responsibility
couldn't stop imagining
the fourteen-year-old girls in his class

Let's just say   they don't have sisters
is what my brother said
when I asked why he had not & would not
introduce me to his fellow soldiers
the week I visited him at his barrack
& so instead we walked out to the middle of a glacier
where it turned out go figure
to be warmer than the parking lot
from which we had started the half mile trek
out of breath through all that sharp blue
my brother's long eyelashes
frozen in tiny icicles
the way he walked behind me
so that I could determine our pace
& he could make sure I didn't slip

THE POET'S FATHER WAKES IN A COLD SWEAT

all those mornings   i washed & chopped strawberries
into pieces that could fit her tiny mouth   all the times
she tucked her icy feet beneath my thigh   & hid
her giggles in my armpit   i knew she was learning
how to be soft   with something large   enough to crush her
what if that was the wrong lesson?   who might she mistake
for the shadow of me?   i should have taught her
how to distrust   anything man-shaped   how to be closed
fist   fast foot   instead   she is slow   to run
when she was small   i signed her up for tee ball   but she stood
in the outfield   singing to the bees   she is tissue
paper folded   & refolded   she walks into traffic
& crowds of men   like she doesn't expect them to destroy her
like she can raise her skinny fingers   & they will yield
bring her back to me   mean & empty night   do not laugh
at this old man   who has let the world steal   what he cannot afford
to lose   return her to me small & trusting   i will try again   i will
teach her   the scowl her brother carries   i will scare her   right
the first time   so she will know   not to venture out again

I AM SEVENTEEN & EVERYONE

is on the subway
or they were   at least
around forty-second
but the Times Square crowds
all shuffled off by thirty-fourth
& the rest of the yawning throng
by fourteenth   which is why
it takes me a minute
to notice him   two seats away
his entire body turned towards mine
unblinking   wolf eyes
making me into wild rabbit
& I am awake
the way a third rail is awake
somewhere beneath my steel
live current   thrumming
his nearness
thicker than a tongue
& by now
the train car is almost empty
at least   I think it is
because I cannot look
because looking
would mean lifting my eyes
& I have committed to gargoyle
he doesn't get to know
that I am working overtime
he is either
going to do something
or he isn't   but I won't
give him the satisfaction
of the fear that will spill
if I shift even an eyelash
so I study the shoes in front of me
I study the litter behind them

I study the metronome of his breath
& the lurch of the car
& review every possible
hypothetical situation I might be in
until he finally rises like a tidal wave
moves past me so slow I age a decade
reaches the platform & turns around
to face me   I feel it
I wait for the doors to close
before I fold like a polite napkin
glance up to his terrifying
full-toothed grin through the glass
if the doors stutter there is enough time
for him to jump back through
but they don't & he doesn't
just keeps his smile bared
stare steady as a pistol
while the train pulls me
towards some other future so
I barely even hear her
when she asks   *you ok?*
because the shoes belong to a woman
her face clear as a calculator
I got you   she doesn't say
though her eyes are a safety net I did not know
had been there this whole time
& I nod my head & deflate—
morning-after prom balloon
leaf in a leaf pile
flute solo in a hurricane

& years from now
when a man I wish would text me back
won't text me back
& I can't help but speed through
every hypothetical situation I might be in
everything he might be feeling
or thinking or saying in his not saying
my friends will laugh gently & tell me
it isn't your job   you know

to always decode men's silence
but how else
could I have made it here
twirling in this patchwork dress
I stitched together
of all my narrow escapes

THE PLACES WE ARE NOT

a man plows his truck
through the crowd
celebrating on the Nice Boardwalk
where my once-love
once insisted
we could make it
all the way through
a triple-layer chocolate mousse
until we were both so full
we could not even bear
to lick our spoons

I text a friend *where are you*
which is code for
please tell me these new deaths
are not yours this time
if I scroll up
I will see the same text I sent her
when Paris was exploding
a few moments
or weeks ago
farther up
the same text she sent me
when I was in lockdown in Jakarta
as the man across town
pulled the pin from his grenade

not yours
this time
is a song that plays so often
I cannot help but memorize the words
are you ok
is the hook
are you ok
is code for *we are not ok*
but please remind me you are breathing

back home
the Black men & women I love
look into mirrors
& wonder if they are loose teeth
in the mouth of an impatient god
are you ok
I text
impotent
please remind me you are breathing   .

I am scared
is not a good enough reason to not get out of bed
the world is falling apart
is not a good enough one either
I ask my mother if growing older
means one wound piled upon another
until we are just a collection of hurt
& she insists *no—*
sometimes somebody gets married
or has a baby

someone teach me a new song please
bring me a spoon
& a mouth to lean across the table for
this time
this time
I am a tangle of string
I am a snow globe of worry
I am a rolodex of fear
they are putting body bags over children on the sidewalk
where I once pushed a bowl away
laughing
I cannot possibly have any more
I am already full

WORTH CELEBRATING

It is possible to make an educated guess
of how many hours you have left with your friends.
I don't recommend the calculus, but the math is waiting for you.
What a fluke that so many of the people I love most
chose the same city to live in. I know how lucky it makes me,
& though nobody wants to say it, it is temporary.
Someone's career will pull them westward,
will want a real backyard for a baby or dog,
will no longer be able to afford this unbearable rent
on an artist's salary. Even if we stick it out,
someone will be the first to let the friendship stale,
will stop answering calls, someone too must be the first to die.
In the meantime, I suggest we fill our pockets with picnics & potlucks.
Phone calls & photographs & songs we know in four-part harmony.
I recommend all of our favorite New York City holidays:
Barista Remembers You By Name Day,
Baby Waves at You on the Subway Day,
Owl or Hawk Spotted in the Park Day,
Pink Week, when trees that have been quiet all winter go full cotton candy.
Did you know someone has kept track
of which humans have survived the highest falls without a parachute
& the unfathomable distances they fell?
The secret is that the majority survived
by accident of good fortune: they landed on snow—
most underestimated of weather,
tiniest fragile memories of water, but together, impenetrable.
Snow, which can mean blindness or burial,
can also, it turns out, in some cases, mean pillow.
Or if not pillow then at least more cushion than casket,
more blanket than grave. I am trying to wash the dishes
& listen to my favorite sound on earth:
my friends laughing around the table in the next room.
& I know it isn't forever, & I know it is selfish,
but I hope we are gathered around the table
when the phone rings, when the water rushes in.

II

BEGINNING IS A SEASON

it is not that I am lonely
it is simply that I cannot stop thinking
about the spice shop
& the owner's heavy overalls
as she climbed up the ladder
& slid along the shelves
her thick accent & midnight hair
the jars of hibiscus flower & peppercorn
I would have stayed there forever if she had let me
cramped inside the crowded aisles
of everything that can be bottled
instead I resisted pushing my hands
into the burlap sack of dried beans
instead she put a living flower bulb that I did not pay for
in a little jar with dirt
told me to take it home & make sure it lived
sometimes beginning is a season
disguised as a challenge
I think
I am asking
for the kind of moment
that hinges open
would make you blush
if you noticed it between the faces of two strangers across the party
a beginning so sharply possible
it exists easiest as memory even while it is still happening
I think
I want to stand in the doorway in between
I understand &
I am understood
& watch them kiss
knowing that to be undone by someone
supposes a past in which you were once done or at least doing
as opposed to being unloved which supposes
nothing at all

ON THE DATING APP I SELECT
FROM THE DROPDOWN MENU TO
INDICATE I TOO LIKE BEACHES

a beach is where I go to stand next to the inconceivable / it is inconceivable
that this sterile void is the closest I get to touching / I touch
the button to indicate that I like men / I like my men like I like my coffee:
more in theory / in theory I am a catch / a catch
is what gets pulled from the ocean gasping
& flailing in the hot sun / the hot sun
burns so I reach for fantasy / fantasy
is a trap door / a trap door is a means to an end / an end
is not supposed to haunt / a haunting is a rejection of ending /
who wants to help me make this haunted house
into a haunted home! (winky face) / a home
is where all your junk is / junk is just litter
that you finally take ownership of / it isn't that complicated /
what if I am addicted to making it complicated /
what if I am addicted to getting in my own way / my own way
is littered with anxiety / litter is what everyone agrees isn't supposed to be there
but I wouldn't recognize myself without the anxiety /
I am just three anxieties in a trench coat—
always the old timey detective, never the femme fatale /
though still protagonist of course / still narrator /
distressingly self-aware / self-*aware*
is not the same as self-*conscious* / which is not the same as self-*centered*
but you're lookin at a three for one, baby! / babies & dogs
are the only topics of conversation at the wedding so I am silent
as a fish / I am inconceivable / hard to swallow /
you can lower your lips to kiss an ocean
but the best you ever leave with is salt

PRAISE MY TINY KITCHEN

which is so small
it is impossible
not to graze each other's bodies
when I am at the stove
& you need to get to the sink
& you do need
to get to the sink
& I do need
you to touch
my shoulder when you pass
& also before you head back
I need your help
because the miso isn't mixing
with the butter & the shallots
the way I imagined it would
when I invited you over
praise the boldness
of who I was yesterday
when I offered to cook you dinner
praise the arrogance
of who I was fifteen minutes ago
attempting a sauce
I've never attempted
which now isn't *emulsifying*
a word I'm only half confident about
but am more confident
that you know
what needs to happen to make it work
praise the sweat
working its way down the back of my shirt
praise the ease
with which you take the spoon
praise the curiosity
of who you were when you learned the chemistry
of what's happening in this saucepan
praise the saucepan

& the shallots & the butter & the miso
that is finally melting
praise the melting
I cannot stop from happening
every time you say something like
coprolite! which you said instinctively
when I showed you the piece
of fossilized poop
that I found on a beach in Scotland
praise who you were
when you learned that word
so you could say it
in my hallway
with such delight
like an exclamation point
that turned me into a cartoon wolf
hitting myself on the head with a wooden mallet
rolling my tongue back in my mouth
praise my human mouth
& whatever it did to get you here
praise this heat
that is July's fault
but also the stove
& the closeness of your neck
praise your neck
& the collar that is holding it
that I touched without thinking
to untuck the corner
so it would lay flat against your chest
praise your chest
& the warmth I can feel
radiating from it
when you pass behind me
praise the way we move
around each other
in the smallness of this kitchen
with no recipe
just sharing
our instincts & eyes
& mouths & hands

& past selves who did
what they needed to do
to make what we are making now
so delicious
so good

KNOWING

You list ten Things You Know to Be True on Monday
& by Thursday half of them have gone overripe on the vine.
You thought you knew something but it turned out you were just hungry.
Just horny. It seemed true for a minute, but then there was a new moon,
a high tide, you thought you knew but it was someone else's knowing
that looked so good on them you thought you'd try it on.
If I had to guess I would say 98% of the time
the answer is *I don't know.* Do I like this?
Did I do that right? Do I want to be here? Is he making a joke? Am I?
Ever-clumsy footing through the haze of this humanness.
Which is why   on the eyelash's chance
that a galaxy nudges left for just a second
& a ray of knowing hits you in the gut
or your heart or wherever you store your maybes,
you have to quit your job. You have to buy the one-way ticket.
You have to tell her you love her, & fast,
before the words mutate into a demand,
when it is still just a fact.
I am not saying let Certainty be your only god.
I have seen the haircuts he demands in his honor.
I am saying if you know, when you know,
you have to honor it. You have to follow it.
You have to give it sunlight & water, a fighting chance. Give it a try.
No matter how inconvenient, how impossible,
how painful, how embarrassing,
no matter the side effects,
the consequences, the fallout, the aftermath,
the risk, the risk, the risk,
all I know is that the exquisite bone buzz
the brief planetary alignment
the simple, most improbable gift of knowing
demands this of you.

DREAMING BOY

In most of the dreams I remember from childhood,
I am a boy. Saving a maiden in a tower
or not saving anyone in particular, but definitely a boy.

For years, when the only language I had were the scraps
tossed to me from the popular kids' table, *lesbian*
seemed as likely an explanation as anything.

What does it mean to dream myself a gender?
What does it mean to hold that secret beneath my tongue?
The first time I kissed a boy, he was so tall, his mouth so soft,

I dreamt of the ocean for weeks. Never in control of my limbs.
Next to him, I seemed like a convincing enough girl.
At least when I was awake. At night, I was Batman.

At night, a fireman. At night, a boy, with muscles in boy places.
& a firm hand. & a direction to run. The first time I kissed a girl,
I didn't like how much our faces melted into each other.

Where was the stubble? I wondered. The hard jaw & cinnamon?
I could not breathe through all her lilac. I dreamt of being lost in the woods.
Of a terrible tidal wave. If I was not a lesbian,

what possible explanation did I have? What words
could I tie around this treacherous heart?
This impossible hunger, this miserable mind?

The first time I meet you, someone says, *Oh, he's definitely gay,*
& maybe that is a confusion I recognize.
The first time we kiss, you tell me to *take it slow.*

I place my hand against your ribcage & you move it away.
I feel like a fourteen-year-old trying to peel off a bra strap.
You spend the night anyway, & we lie next to each other, just breathing,

my hands inches away from your boxers, twitching against the covers.
The next day, you make the bed & fold all of my clothes while I am at class.
You learn to play the harp & sing me songs while you play.

For my birthday, you bake me a triple layer cake, wake up early to ice it.
I watch your shirtless torso push icing through a tube,
I have never loved a body the way I love yours in that moment.

You pick flowers on your way to work, leave bouquets in every room.
When you dance, the walls lean to get closer to you.
When I finally ask you if you might want to date men,

I hold my breath while you think about it for a long, quiet minute.
I haven't met one I'd like to date yet, you say. *& for right now,*
I'm pretty in love with you, if that's ok. & just like that,

I do not crave language that I always thought I needed.
& just like that, somewhere a hand reaches backwards into a
faraway dream & says, *Come on, then. We've got a maiden to save.*

I guess what I am saying is you make me feel like a boy.
Like the boy I have always been. At night, I climb trees
& wear cargo shorts. I scale buildings & build fires.

When I wake, I am curled around your back, the happiest big spoon
in the drawer. You are naked & heavy-breathing, the man I love.
I hold your body like the gift it is, & safely sink back into dreams.

NEW YEAR'S EVE

the fifth floor walk-up & the river of hallway shoes
& the fogged up windows & the kitchen of bottles
& the turned up volume & the drowned out laughter
& the friends of friends & the liquored flirting
& the smudged eyeliner & the sequined dresses
& the sardined torsos & the denim boners
& the remote scramble & the chanted countdown
& the sloppy kisses & the bedroom turned coat-room
& the mountain of jackets & the dearth of floorspace
& the locked door & his hurried hands & our tangled giggles
& his easy buckle & his familiar shape & the ignored knocking
& our ragged breaths & our knitted fingers
& the romance of the calendar & the story forming
& the view from above & the way I'd retell it
& even now   every hurt   that came later   cannot reach me there

TABLE GAMES

At restaurants, our favorite game was to touch
an object on the table & casually offer a pun
into the existing conversation.

Touching the pepper grinder, I might say, *You crack me up.*
Then you would graze your knife & declare,
That's a sharp observation. I would hold the water glass & caution,

Don't get too full of yourself, & you would
nod seriously & apologize as you signed the check,
You're write, I'm sorry.

Back & forth we went, eyes shifting from napkin
to soup spoon, considering the tabletop like a chess board,
giggling at our secret from the waiters.

The best, of course, was when a new object
was introduced to the table. Something surprising
or difficult to maneuver into wordplay,

something that left us both staring hard & silent,
racing each other's brains to the cleverest quip.
You were always faster than I.

I could not keep up with your lightning mind,
but rejoiced, instead, in the satisfaction it gave you
to beat me to the punchline, to see you beam at your own wit,

& then at me, your favorite audience.
Food always tastes more delicious when you feel victorious.
Maybe this is why people like to hunt.

The day you broke up with me, you took me to Whole Foods for lunch.
This is a pain, because there are so many of them in the city
& they each look the same, so now every one feels like the scene of the crime.

After you told me that you had forgotten my name
in so many other mouths,
I said, *It's ok,* & held your hand while you cried.

If I had been just a little bit faster, I would have reached
for the cheap paper napkin holder & said,
Thank you for dispensing this knowledge to me.

It would not have been one of my stronger puns,
but it might have made you laugh,
which was still what I wanted most of all in that moment.

I could have knocked on the counter between us
& said, *Let's table this for later,*
or reached for a plastic spoon & winked,

I guess I was more disposable than I thought.
Maybe a nod to the takeout box—
You sure kept this information contained!

I can't believe you kept a lid on this for so long,
as I take a swig of water,
I'll bet it was really hard to keep bottled up!

Maybe I could have punned my way out of the store,
shouting a line about every product on the shelves,
throwing them to the ground as I wound my way

backwards through each aisle to the exit.
Can you imagine the response I would have gotten?
Employees wiping their hands on their green aprons,

pausing from shelving the quinoa,
turning to see the Crazy Pun Lady go out with a bang.
I could have delivered one final zinger,

shouting, *I've never been so beet-rayed!*
as I pushed over the entire display of violet roots,
causing every shopping-cart-wielding mom

to burst into sympathetic applause as I bowed my way out.
Actually, I doubt anyone would have even noticed.
I am sure wilder things happen in Whole Foods all the time.

Instead I said *it's ok.*

Which was the opposite of what I meant.
I meant *it's not ok.*
I meant *why?*

I meant *please don't leave me.*
I meant *I have loved you for five years.*
I meant *who will I play with when the waiters aren't looking?*

Who will I race to impress with my banter?
Who will smile at me when he reaches the punchline first,
delighted that he has won?

PULLING A SARAH

When the beer is finished, the sun almost rising,
the party melting into yawns,
instead of just sleeping over, Aubie always opts
to drive home through the night
to wake in his own bed. He has done it so many times
through the years, we all know what it means
when someone says, *I think I might need to pull an Aubie,*
just as everyone knows that *pulling a Josh* means
staying up 'til dawn to do a friend a favor,
even & especially if it isn't necessary,
even & especially if nobody asked him to.
Everyone is too polite to tell me what *pulling a Sarah* means,
but they laugh when I say I have forgiven all my exes
to clear out enough space for my grudges against theirs.
Not just their exes. Apologies in advance if I ever get the chance
to tell Katelyn's father what I think of him,
good luck to Emily's once-hookup if I catch him in the street alone.
The last time someone broke my heart,
before I lowered myself into the grief well with no ladder,
I let him cry into the fake fur collar of my thrift store coat,
joked around to cheer him, even hugged him before he left.
It wasn't until I heard the venom in Katelyn's voice,
He doesn't get to treat you like that,
nobody gets to treat you like that,
that it even occurred to me I had a heart worth protecting.
I ask my therapist why I can't get angry on my own behalf,
but it is not really anger I am asking about.
Like when I am on the phone with Sophia,
who has known me since we were bundles strapped to our mothers' chests,
who I don't even have to see to know she is pushing fingers through
the wings of her greying hair as she listens to me unravel
my long list of failures, my evidence for self-loathing,
who waits until I am done before she says softly,
I don't like the way you are talking about my friend.
& I don't have to respond for her to stay on the phone,
& she doesn't have to say any more for me to know she is still there.

HITTING ROCKS INTO USELESS BAY

Once, in Puerto Rico, I held on to a rock ledge for forty-five minutes,
refusing to jump into the lagoon below.

Friends shouted encouragement & strangers offered kind advice,
until finally the man I loved crawled up the rock face & stood behind me

coaxing, *This is not a metaphor.*
He said this because he knew that I had already found a way

to equate this failure with all other failures.
Knew that my mind is a tangle of labyrinths

with unwarranted symbolism hiding around every stubborn corner.
I laughed because it was so accurate, & also

because if I died going down, those would be the last words I heard.
Instead, I jumped & survived, & that night in bed he wrapped his arms

around me & whispered, *It was a metaphor. Me. I am the metaphor.*
I showed up because I believe in you. Because I love you &

I knew that you could do it. Because I will scale anything when you need me.
Because you did need me. & he was already asleep before I could answer,

leaving me to stalk my own hallways for the meanings
of the clutched rock, the shaking legs, the racing heart,

the fall, the smack, the coldest shock,
& the man who climbed up to tell me to let go.

Not even a year later, he has moved into someone else's body,
& I am on a beach in Washington.

I have come here to hide from my sorrow,
to try & write poems that do not lead back to him.

Instead, I find myself watching a pack of young men
throw rocks into the air, before swinging bats of driftwood

& smashing them over the water, the *thwack* & *pop* & *plunk*
echoing up & down the otherwise empty beach.

& yes, the name of this beach is *Useless Bay.*
& yes, the young men are swinging as hard as they can, of course.

& yes, it is twilight,
& yes, I am all alone,

& I do not want these metaphors.
I would give them all back if I could.

Even if it meant a rainstorm would forever be just a rainstorm,
a ladybug on my arm simply that.

Still, I would trade it for this relentless weight of meaning.
This unfair promise of always finding pattern where there need not be any.

Let the young men be just young men, & not my heart, forever swinging.
Let the water be just water & not the vast loneliness.

Let the driftwood be driftwood, let the bay be unnamed,
let the sunset not be my time running out,

but only the hour of the day,
only an indication that the bugs will soon be out,

that the young men will pull on their sweatshirts,
that I should be heading home.

AN ADDRESS I'LL FORGET

The woman who has agreed
to let me borrow a place on her couch
is pointing out local sights: the parking lot
for weekly farmer's markets, the basketball court.
As we pass by Chapman Elementary School
she tells me of the *vaux swift*: a bird
that stays in flight so constantly,
it barely lands to make nests
& even eats while still mid-air.
But every year around August,
the birds start their long journey down
to South American warmth, &
on their way they stop here,
at the chimney of Chapman.
Since the 1980s the swifts
have chosen this brick tower
as a replacement for the firs
they once roosted in, now gone
to greedy hands & urban sprawl.
A tricky riddle cleverly solved:
standing hollow trees, now rare,
are substituted with this
great infertile smokestack.
The school even turned off the heat
despite Portland's cool September days,
so that the birds can visit undisturbed.
As the sun dips itself in chilly evening,
for what feels like a communal inhale,
the sky fills with flapping shadow,
& like coffee grounds whirlpooling
towards a sink drain, the swifts
funnel themselves into their
vertical hallway, to rest until dawn.
You should come back in September,
my host says dreamily,
it is really something to see.
She says the whole neighborhood

gets into it, dragging lawn chairs & blankets
to watch the nightly arrival,
like a confetti cannon in reverse.
I look at the giant dormant cigar & nod,
picturing the thermoses & warm hats,
the lawn perfumed with rotting leaves,
the sun sinking
over Portland's sleepy roofs,
poking honey fingers through every
window & moss-covered stoop.
I imagine the head nods to neighbors,
the handshakes & pleasantries exchanged,
a joke about the local high school's
most recent basketball loss, & then—
all faces turning to greet
the tiny harbingers of Autumn,
the birds whose bodies seem always in motion,
who perhaps might not
have been designed to stop,
if you believe in such designs,
who might never have paused at all
if not for the tradition of this edifice,
if not for the muscle memory
of this portal to better days.
Yes, I say, *I'd love to see that.*
But she & I both know the truth:
that September is hundreds of days
from now & by then
I will already be in some other pocket
of the world, dragging my suitcase
towards someone else's doorstep,
a house that isn't mine, an address I'll forget
after a couple days, & Portland
will be just a distant evening,
feathers falling through smokeless air.

ORANGE

The monks who are waiting at my gate at JFK might not be monks,
but they are all wearing orange robes, orange sandals,
they are rolling orange carry-on bags, & one of them
even has an orange neck pillow already on his shoulders,
in preparation for this flight to Dallas. I know the rules
about photographing people you don't know, but forgive me,
I snap the shot, so I can send it to my mother & make her day.

My mother won't say that she gave up photography to raise children,
but it is true that she used to be a professional printer
with a life of image-making & then stopped to fill her arms
with babies & then toddlers & then children & then
the things teenagers handed her when we refused to be held any longer.
You might think that a woman who spent hours inhaling chemicals
& grueling over various sinks & under various lights
to create a perfectly balanced image
would begrudge a technology that imitates it,
but you haven't met my mother. This is a woman who loves New York
more than she loves any human alive or dead.
Every day she walks through the same shitty city as the rest of us,
but when I return with a mouth full of complaints about the weather,
the subway, the tourists, she remains an endless scroll of wonders
of things she insists could only happen in New York.
So when my childhood friend James teaches her to use the app we all use,
she isn't angry, but amazed. *This would have taken so much work
in the darkroom,* she says. *Now it's just a button, it's like magic.*

When James & I were little, his favorite color was orange,
& my mother loved this fact, found it strange & marvelous—
this little boy willing to forgo firetrucks & Power Rangers,
claiming the untouched reject of the crayon box, preferring
the traffic cone, the citrus fruit. To practice using the app
& get her photography sea legs under her again,
she photographs orange objects around the house & on the street.
She only has two followers—James & me—but every caption is the same:
Orange for James, & she wanders the city as wide-eyed as always,

stopping strangers with, *Excuse me, I noticed your wonderful orange bag*
your hat   your construction vest   that's my nephew's favorite color,
may I photograph it? Never mind that he isn't her nephew,
never mind that it makes him sound six & not thirty, which he is,
this is the way she has always moved through New York,
in search of bright morsels she can bring home to share.

In Dallas, I wait for my bag at the carousel,
& a man in a corduroy jacket approaches,
asks me if I am Sarah Kay. When I say yes,
he says, *My priests know your poetry & thought that it was you!*
motions over his shoulder to the men in orange behind him,
but when I wave he says, *I'm sorry. Because of their religious vows,*
they are not permitted to communicate with someone of your gender,
but they asked me to tell you that they wish you continued success.

Days later, a new email through my website:
We hope to have not offended you by not meeting in person to appreciate your work
& also pray that your poetry lights up minds, smiles & souls
of all those searching for meaning; that your beauty with words
be not just a trained art but a reflection of who you wish to be.
& then an offering of a poem in Sanskrit, which roughly translates:
On bearing fruits, trees bend, become humble
with newly gathered water, clouds hang very low…
this is the nature of the benevolent.

I used to think this was a story about coincidence
or about the invisible thread of poetry that so many people are holding on to,
even & especially people who may not have anything else in common.
But I think it is actually a story about my mother.
How she didn't have to take a photograph for thirty years
to make a camera of a daughter,
or at least teach her that the way you notice
can be a weapon or an act of love,
that color blooms through every city,
whether you see it or don't, whether you *seek* it or don't,
so why not seek? Why not see?
Why not ask yourself: who am I looking for?

SONNET FOR POP

cartoon giant who taught me how to hold court & host dinner
happiest stoner photographing a dying dahlia in the living room
echoingest laugh in the deli line, *Morning, Brother, the regular!*
who asks me, *Am I going to cry?* before I read him each poem
who doesn't speak Hebrew but hears his dead father's voice in every prayer
who weeps his soggy bass louder than the cantor
no art school, no college, just a light-chaser
lookin for fresh fodder, soft focus, sweet banter
who misses my call beneath Ellington blasting
I swore I'd never write a poem that made my father feel left out
always a door unlocked, a table set, no wasting
a chance to share a sandwich, a dumb pun, a walkabout
a secret, a polaroid, a car ride, a shore
a sunflower, forever, & later, more

SHARPSHOOTERS

On our way back from a barbecue in Brooklyn,
we drive past an old building's fading wall,
paint peeling like sunburnt shoulders.
My parents see it at the same time & pull over,
no conversation necessary. Within seconds
they are lens-deep in rust,
ten feet apart, cameras raised, eyes searching,
already worlds away from the car behind them
& their sighing daughter in the backseat.
These parallel lines that made me,
who have interrupted every family road trip
to investigate a pile of scrap metal off the highway
or the ivy reclaiming a farmhouse,
the way an abandoned train car exhales into a field.
My father pauses to ask my mother a question,
& she takes a look at his side of the wall,
their voices softer than I can grasp, two fishermen
curious about each other's full buckets,
their many hooks sunk into golden hour shadows.
I knew kids whose car rides did not include
detours to ruins, whose parents
did not take art-making seriously,
or else they did, & too seriously—
were smug & pretentious about taste,
competitive about accomplishment & recognition.
But my parents simply love making photographs:
for themselves, for each other,
to see the deteriorating world
from as many angles as the light provides,
to admire each other's catch
& linger a little longer than the rest of us,
tapping our feet impatiently in the car.

ALLOW ME JUST THIS ONE

Despite how carefully I have buried
my once-love's voice,
how well I disposed of the images,
sometimes a fragment still floats back
& when I am exhausted
from a long day of the world
treating me exactly the way I fear I deserve
& I am too tired to fight myself,
my heart unclenches enough to remember

Oregon in the soft rain,
my head against the rental car window,
his singing easing my heavy eyelids,
until I shot up & said, *stop the car.*
He called to me just once
but I was already gone,
seatbelt left swinging before the car was in park,
consumed by my vision, scouring the brush.
Eventually I found them: a procession
of overgrown cars worshiping the Oregon soil,
beckoning me like a splintered lighthouse.
Shrines to the Gods of Decay.
Moss & leaves & metal & tire.
Paint cracked into a map. Fractured windshield
slicing a tree into a forest of reflections.
Bumpers erupting pine needles. A motor escaping its steel.
I don't know how long I feverishly photographed
before I thought to apologize & beg
for a few more shivering minutes,
attempt to explain the history of the ritual,
to confide that I learned to write
the way my parents photograph—looking for light,
running an eager hand across a moment for as long as it allows.

& here, I confess, is what I come back to:
a few yards away, stationed over a spilled engine,
turning his own camera this way & that—

my once-love, who asked for no explanation,
abandoned the day's plans with ease,
questioned neither my departure nor my pursuit,
& left my private reverie unpunctured
until he saw me lift my head &
scan the junkyard once more,
nodding my satisfaction.
He led me back to the car, turned on the heat,
& pulled onto the highway,
singing as the rain resumed.

& even while it all shrinks ever-smaller in the rearview,
I forgive her, the me who returns there,
sifting through the ruins of our time together
for what trace of beauty still shines through.

THE CHURCH OF COUPLEDOM

has evangelists so savvy,
even at your most chimerical,
before you can even read,
they have made a disciple out of you.
Yes, through the obvious modes:
the princess stories & your own parents
& the way even the moon is defined first by her devotion,
but the Church is in the water, the air,
the mist of longing you inhale—
one lung has never seen the other
but is still a believer,
suspects it is only half-enough,
senses that somewhere beyond its borders
there must be another reaching in the same direction.
You absorb the Church through your pores.
It swims through you,
until the fate of lone wolves
& spinster witches need not even be stated,
you carry it behind your eyes (also paired).
& if you do work overtime
to wipe away the propaganda gunk
that accumulates again at every waking
& clings even through your dreams,
you might, for a short time, escape—

finally confident that the jig is up,
that you see the way
thunder & lightning are not lovers,
are not chasing each other across heavens,
are, in fact, one thing:
the way   we are, each
splintered into louder & silent times,
brighter & invisible parts,
& only the speed at which
we decide to share them
(& with whom) depends.
In fact, to think you are *alone*
is to lack imagination—

is to fail to see the ivy, the lampposts,
the eyelashes, the poems,
the Great Loves & siblings you have
already been blessed with—
how surrounded by love you are!
How stupid with wealth!

But the Church will catch you slipping.
Send you someone with a slick mouth
who smells like possibility, & there you go again,
embarrassingly knocking on the wooden doors,
fumbling your meager alms to see
if there is still time for your salvation,
still time to join the sanctified
in the holy land of partnership,
& yes, of course, I know, purpose
becomes clearer when you have someone else to live for.
But I also know for a fact

there was once a time
when I was still small enough
to slip between the fingers of this inherited quest
& tipped my nose from tide pool to tide pool,
mouth an open cave of awe,
each small crater of water an entire universe
I could stargaze into, teeming with stories I could
dip my fingers in, the earthly aliens of salt water endless
& visible & silent & bright & loud.

EACH OF US HERE

Call me arrogant if you want,
but I have written enough poems to know
I can sit in the basement of my own insecurities & not flinch.
Can flick on the light & give others a small tour,
have a knack, even, for guiding folks into their own
dimly lit corners, know what to do with my face & hands
when they bravely offer their softest parts in poem or conversation.
If there was a girl scout badge for ease with human vulnerability
I think I could earn it, or already have, but nothing prepared me
for the hallway at the fertility clinic
where the chairs are close enough
that our elbows might touch if we let them splay
but there is no splaying here. No touching.
Never an empty seat. We all face the same direction which is to say
our phones, lifelines to any other hallway that isn't this one,
eye contact impossible, only the most peripheral glimpses
of pearls & purses & backpacks & baseball hats,
each of us here because something has not gone
the way we were led to believe it would go
or was supposed to go or would have gone if we were normal
or right or on time & there's no way around it, both the thoughts
& also the hallway. You have to sit here until they call your name
& sometimes you have a name that is common
so they add the first letter of your last name to clarify which means
when the nurse whispers into the microphone to summon me
they are calling my whole name out for all to hear,
& I am not ashamed but definitely aware
of the tiniest sliver of anonymity afforded everyone else
that slides off me like a loin cloth when I rise.
It is a beckoning I asked for. Blood I give freely,
body I offer in exchange for answers. But they don't have answers.
They have probabilities. & known averages & studies
& a hallway of girl scouts showing up
a few minutes early for our Hope Appointments.

Hey, I went to the Vulnerability Hallway & everybody knew you,
is what I would say to myself to make me laugh.
But it would also be a lie because I did go & nobody knew me,
my aloneness louder than it had ever been,
each of our breaths too busy being held, each of their silences a mercy.

TO WHOEVER BROKE INTO THE RENTAL CAR & STOLE MY VIBRATOR

Perhaps I deserve this.
After all, wasn't my very ownership of this   magic wand

an act of theft? Demanding something that isn't yours,
that you have only coveted   through shop windows

& computer screens,   the throbbing power
you are not supposed to have;   I too am guilty.

I too have dreamed of owning what was not meant for me.
I too have lusted after the high   of a wide stance on a crowded subway,

the buzz   of a boardroom that will look me in the eyes—
who can be blamed for that desire?

I apologize if you were misled. It was dark & raining.
You must have thought those boxes were full   of electronics or something

of value instead of the poetry books that greeted you,
how embarrassing. You left them all behind. I know because I counted.

I left them drying in a friend's apartment, the ruined pages cracked & curling.
You took my rain jacket. Smart. You took a pair of jeans,

some underwear, my camera (this, at least, you can sell),
& then I imagine you slid your hand   along the lining of the suitcase

until your fingers came to curl   around that coy cylinder—
I am sure that even in the downpour you knew what it was.

I wonder if you took it without pausing. If it was an afterthought
or the Crown Jewel, whether it redeemed the waste

of the broken window, the stupid poetry books.
Did you pause to consider the body it once soothed?

The drawers it was hidden in? The roommates it embarrassed?
I wonder   if you use it. I wonder

what it means if you do. I will tell you one thing though:
sometimes when a man interrupts me   or his hands

are thunder claps that roll in unexpected,
when the broken glass & soggy poetry   of me

is not enough   to stop his engine, sometimes
there is a rush of blood to my face. A tightening of muscles.

Sometimes I go lightheaded & my hands fist.
Sometimes I envy   your ability to take.

III

UNRELIABLE

Where is my prize for most unreliable narrator?
I would never lie to you, but I lie to me all the time.
I say, *Look at that bird, this childhood memory,*
that light falling across his body in the steam,
& say, Boom. A stone Truth. A Poem. & you trust me.
You trace your finger along the constellation I'm insisting
into existence & let my rickety astrology determine the weather.
But this is all dominoes.
I am just trying to place enough words between now & The End
to trick The End into coming later.
I slip single doses of myself into the pockets of everyone I love,
worried about serving sizes, hoping they do not sour once I'm gone.
I spent thirty-two years in New York City
& every metaphor is stacked with taxi cabs & subways.
I spent two weeks in the woods & suddenly every poem swelled
with rhododendrons & the smell of firewood.
I am the most porous sponge that ever sponged.
I throw myself off every emotional cliff
& build a pogo stick on the way down.
I am not an optimist but I play one in the group chat.
I don't know who I think I need absolution from,
but I carry around a shiny report card everywhere I go just in case.
I thought I wanted a boyfriend but I actually wanted an audience.
My father carried dried mushrooms from the market
to the wood table on the front porch so he could watch
the way the late afternoon sun made patterns in their crackled skin
& called my mother out of the house so she could stand next to him
& look at it too. They were so excited they forgot to close
the screen door & the bugs made a home of the kitchen.
I have never accomplished anything in my life
other than the seven mile run to the lighthouse.
This land—someone else's, this language—someone else's,
even the ocean of fear that pours out of me—an inheritance,
or if not an inheritance then a reaction, a riverbank
formed out of a rushing past I had nothing to do with.
I make a phone call & when you don't pick up
the whole house falls down around me.

I am the center of my own dramatic universe & it appalls me.
In my dream, from somewhere down a hallway of locked doors, a voice asks,
What if you aren't as bad as you suspect you are?
What if you'll never be as good as you ache?
& then, softer, in the kind of whisper that wouldn't even fog the glass,
What if what you are is boring
& alive, what are you going to do then?

NATURE VS. NURTURE

Of course I cannot stop looking at photographs
of the sand in Okinawa, each grain
a perfect star, which is actually exoskeleton
of marine protozoa that lived
on the ocean floor & ended up there.
I want to slip my hands in the beach of tiny vertebrae,
make a constellation of backbone snowflakes in my palm.
The first blizzard of the year is a fine time to discover
that everyone in my neighborhood apparently owns a sled,
the park now flooded with bright mittens
thrown in the air like wedding bouquets.
All my conversations involve fertility:
who wants kids, who doesn't,
who is trying, who won't,
meanwhile the moon
has been gradually moving away from us for years.
Not ghosting, just the slowest electric slide through space,
& shame on us for not noticing until now.
Or noticing & forgetting,
remembering again & getting sad.
Shame on us for thinking we were unleavable,
what with the mess we've made,
shame on us for continuing to put the moon in our poems
like an ex we can't stop bringing up in conversation,
shame on us for using the royal We.
I wrote a poem about a bird made of birds
& now strangers send me news stories
about flamingos standing in the shape of a flamingo,
a shark strapped with gps who draws a shark on the map,
a shark made of shark. That means there are people
I have never met who see something unbelievable,
smile, shake their heads, & the next thing on their mind is me,
which isn't the worst way to live in other people's heads.
One reason to have a kid that isn't the worst reason,
is that at a certain point it becomes increasingly rare
to experience anything for the first time,
so I really luxuriate

over a mouthful of fruit I've never met before.
I take it back. New isn't hard to find,
but the firsts from here on out start to get Cathedral scary.
First diagnosis, first divorce, first funeral,
while the lasts slip away from us gradually, like a moon,
often without notice,
last baby tooth, last kiss, last look, last breath.
There I go saying *us* again,
like my melancholy is a shared responsibility.
In every photograph of me in love,
my head is tilted to the side,
& I have since been told
that animals only show their neck
as a sign of submission.
Somewhere through my lineage on both sides,
an ancestor got on a boat—
something I can't do without
immediately giving up my insides & my will to live.
When my therapist asks if I'm the only person in my family
who struggles with anxiety, I nod my head
& straighten my spine.

TSUBU

(Because their parents were their parents) my mother & her siblings learned to eat rice with chopsticks & the bowl's rim at a close distance to their mouths which meant that an errant grain would frequently end up on someone's cheek in the midst of the shoveling & it turns out there is a word in Japanese for this single rebel grain which my mother & her siblings knew (because their grandparents were their grandparents) & the word is *tsubu* (which is one of the only words I know in Japanese because when I was young & eating rice the way I learned to eat it (because my mother is my mother) she would sometimes giggle *tsubu!* & point at my cheek which is frankly kinder but less funny than what her siblings used to do (which was not say anything at all but rather lift a single grain & silently place it on their own faces in the exact same place where she had missed her own until she looked up & noticed their stifled snickers) so I do not blame my mother for saying she *never felt the need to be a mother after being the eldest of those five* —which is what she always says when having children comes up in conversation— (which it does a lot these days) & perhaps this is why she is so great at parenting (so many people—myself included—because she has had so much practice) but is not particularly interested in mothering (something entirely different which I know because I have been bigger than my mother since I was ten & have not been mothered in the way that I imagine other people sometimes are mothered—with a cooing

voice & hair-stroking—which my mother
would never do because my curls have al-
ways baffled her (even when I was a child)
because her hair is pin straight & down to
her butt unless it is piled on top of her head
which it was for the brain surgery for which
everyone was worried they would shave her
entirely (even though she was excited about
the possibility of a mohawk but instead
came out with only the back shaved) to
make room for the scar like a giant number
seven (which is less than the number of
nights I spent at her bedside where she in-
troduced me to every nurse as her daughter
Sarah: Worry Wart while I called her only
homie or *pal* as though addressing a friend
might keep me from losing a mother) but
she was not lost & very lucky & now foggy
& confined to small phrases (as though sit-
ting inside a robot) though deep down still
my mother whom I feed small spoonfuls of
congee rice porridge (which I flavored with
furikake that my father brought to the hos-
pital from home because my mother is my
mother) & through the valium haze she
asks me if I remember the story of the
monks who only need three grains of rice
to survive their journey but I don't which
annoys her until a few days later she re-
members & tells me that the monks only
need three grains because the first grain is
for nourishment & survival & the second
grain is for abundance & gratitude & the
third grain is for sharing & the fact that she
remembers the story is a good sign but the
best sign is the next morning when I come
in to find her awake & upright in bed wav-
ing a piece of paper she has written on in
pencil that she demanded from the night
nurse so she could tell me that she figured
out that a fourth grain of rice is necessary: *a*

tsubu! which makes her laugh & me cry when she hands me the paper where she has worked it all out—that the tsubu is necessary so we have humor at ourselves so we know we have no control but it is ok we know nothing it is what gives us curiosity & wonder & serendipity which (because her daughter is her daughter) she makes into a pun—*Sarah dippity*—& then adds: *not worry wart, trust universe.*

JELLO

I hand my mother her fiftieth Jello cup of the week
& she tells me I should write a poem about Jello.
She knows that I will not,
knows I do not respond to instructions
from anyone about what poems I *should* write,
not even my own instructions most days.
When I thought she was dying
I promise my brain was a no-poetry zone.
It was also a no-feelings zone.
I have an advanced degree in
compartmentalization,
can juggle all means of apocalypse
with the padlocks firmly in place.
I swear I have never started writing
a poem in the middle of a kiss or a crisis,
promise that I always said, *just a second!*
when I heard the poem knocking.
But I need to confess
that once it became clear
this particular moment was not her last,
the poem began jiggling the doorknob,
pushing its way in on the taxiride home from my nightshift,
my breath still ripe with hospital.
My mother asks for Jello, says, *Jello is my friend,*
says, *You need   write poem   about Jello.*
One time years ago
when I was frustrated with a poem, my mother
told me, *Missy. Poems are like children.*
If you are patient & listen, they show you
who they want to be.
I open the Jello for my mother.
She gives me my instructions.
My mother opens the poem for me.
The poem gives me my instructions.
The poem says, Be honest.
This is where you put
everything you wish you could wrap your arms around—

encircled with a ribbon of language,
neatly-packaged, handed off.
Nice poem you got there.
Would be a shame if death was inevitable &
you couldn't fit your arms around it.
Would be a shame if you only knew one coping mechanism.
Tell God that my mother
cannot possibly be back in the hospital
because I already finished the poem
in which she survives.

THE POET WAKES IN A COLD SWEAT

You want wand but your hand only speaks crowbar.
You want lineage but create accidental prophecy instead.
The nurse's uniform fits but you keep missing the vein,
until the blood pools blue beneath the skin.
You watched someone skip a stone
across a lake's face, & the fact that something
so clumsy & heavy in the pocket could fly
in the right hands, made you pledge
to summon & hoard & practice & study,
until you too could make a sunset bloom on the right cheeks,
could mend the quilt's tear with a needle sexed by the right thread.
But you have worshiped at the wrong temple,
made sacrifices to the wrong god.
Everybody knows you could have gotten
a better exchange rate at the image bank.
You think when the nightgown of memory
slips from the shoulders of this moment
anybody will remember your words?
They will be at home around the fire.
You will be stacking rocks in your little piles,
watching the maze grow higher, convinced
that because you placed them,
you know how to get back out.

KUCHISABISHII

There is a word in Japanese
for when you're not hungry
but you eat because your mouth is lonely

If you do not have a companion it is assumed
you must be looking for one
Nobody will believe otherwise

I do not want to alarm you
but I have traveled through time
know that sounds like a line in a poem

but is the plainest way I know to say it
Once in the middle of a kiss
I arrived inside myself

in the past
in the middle of some other kiss
& when I returned was disoriented

pulled my face back to find out
whose beard this was
To be clear

it isn't that I forgot who I was kissing
& mistook him for a man I once loved
I am talking about time travel

I am not trying to sound impressive
I don't have any control over it
It used to only drop me off in the past

for a short visit
sometimes just long enough
for a brisk walk along the river in a sensible sweater

sometimes only long enough to catch a glimpse
of a moment I was certain about anything
These days it drops me off in

well there's no other way to say it but
the future &
I do not want to alarm you

but I have reached the very end
tipped my body as far forward as I can
the way you might lean off the edge of a stage in the dark

I have never been a person looking for an exit
but I have seen it now
the exit I mean

that's about as close as I can get with words
it's very big it stretches & stretches
but not like a sharp line

or a line at all no edge to run a hand against just open
it is ok to be scared but I am not
I am sorry

There are already so many things I have done for the last time
I am sorry sometimes I forget to be here because I am there
at the exit instead

Sorry sometimes there
feels closer than any other future
& I know I know   I get it

there is no right way to be single
but I'm doing it wrong
I know those of you wrapped around someone warm

can't even imagine winter
sometimes even I have a hard time believing me
when I promise that I'm full

RETURN TO USELESS BAY

On the drive from the airport
an eight-minute hurricane
knocked out all the electricity on the island
so the ferry docked in darkness,
a thousand treacherous branches
obstacle-coursing the roads
which the headlights
made a horror movie.
By the time I reached the cabin,
the storm had knocked
in the windows so they wouldn't close,
so I made a fire & slept in my winter coat
while the wind & sea
aired out their disagreements &
I know you asked for less metaphors.
Requested none, if I remember correctly.
Promised to be content with the neutral to sad circumstances
of your life if you could be spared
the punishment of symbolism
creeping in to whisper insult to injury.
But baby, metaphor is distance.
Nothing rocketships you farther faster
than a sleek image plucked from your ample arsenal,
no armor thicker than pointing
your poetry finger & yelling, *Look over there!*
It feels so much better to say you climbed
your way up from the bottom of the grief pit,
than to stand in the mundane facts of your aloneness.
You know that. You wrote the poem.
What other ladder did you have?
I want to tell you that the part that won't let you go
is the part that offers a way out: the ladybug,
the rainstorm, this fire you made
with your two good hands,
it all might be nothing, of course.
But what if it's something?
What if it's worth waiting to see.

THE MINISTER OF LONELINESS

In Japan, more people died by suicide in the month of October 2020 than had died from COVID-19 in all of 2020 up to that point. In response, Japan instituted a new position of government: a minister of loneliness.

The minister of loneliness has abolished email. He is installing tin cans on every windowsill, with a piece of string to someone else's window. Not several, just one. Each person, of course, does not need a lot of people to speak to, just the one, but the one must be reliable, must be available when needed, we are employing a buddy system now. Every day is a field trip to the Adulthood Museum, & we don't go home until everyone has been accounted for. The way you find your buddy is a nation-wide game of Guess Who, where you sing the song that is always stuck in your head, describe the movie you can't get through without crying, the hardest you've ever laughed, the outfit you wish you could pull off, & the only person who can spot you is the one you are assigned. All of Japan is a ball of string now. The economy has ground to a halt. Productivity is entirely impossible. Sometimes you go to talk into the can on your windowsill & a knot in the string accidentally gives you someone else's conversation, the fading fabric of someone else's loneliness evaporating into the air between buildings. You are allowed to eavesdrop but so is everyone else. The minister of loneliness has moved all kindergartens to the ground floor of elderly assisted living centers. There are daily story hours. Animal shelters across the street. The minister of loneliness has not abolished Valentine's Day but has employed a nation-wide Bring Enough For the Class Regulation, & nobody goes home empty-handed. The minister of loneliness has prescribed therapy for everyone, daily walks through the many gardens, opportunities for meditation by a brook, in the rain, under falling blossoms, or along a snowy river bank, depending on the season. He has commissioned musicians, actors, & poets to create concerts & radio plays & poetry readings to be pumped across the knotted tin can radio lines. Every evening, when you order dinner for one, the person who delivers it arrives with an appropriate ability & comfort-level dance instruction video & two hours to spare. Grieving is encouraged, & art-making is rampant, but because of the knots, sometimes when you are expecting a visit from a grief counselor, the dance partner food delivery arrives instead. Sometimes they are the same person. The minister of loneliness isn't tired. He is the most popular man in the country. He has a crush on a middle school teacher across town, & everyone eavesdrops to hear the way he stumbles when she answers, everyone is on the edge of their seats. Everyone forgets about dying because they can't wait to find out what happens next, everyone has opinions. The minister has to start a hotline where people can call in to tell him their thoughts. The tin cans rattle nonstop. The minister is grateful for the advice, but is nervous his crush will hear the commotion. He is nervous she prefers quiet, but he does not know for sure yet. He does not know what she is thinking, does not know how she spends her Saturdays or how she prefers her tea or whether she likes to walk in the rain but he likes wondering. When nobody is paying attention, when the windowsills are quiet, late at night awake, he does like to wonder.

QUIET

you used to stay up later than the whole apartment
the whole building   often what felt like the whole city
just to see if quiet would show up & when it did
you honored it with poems   became so charmed by it
called yourself a devotee   oh you *must* have quiet
you insisted you *must*   the poems won't arrive without it
how could you possibly have a pet
with their panting & tail-wagging away your precious quiet
nobody else understood! with their music-listening
& their love-making & their horn-honking
but the quiet was your comrade   your ally
until it turned on you   at the wedding
where you were the only unmarried woman over thirty
& every conversation was about babies or dogs
the quiet in your mouth souring by the hour
the friend who used to reach out daily   stops
& the quiet that moves in
takes up more space than their body ever did   & you
cannot believe quiet would betray you this way
you who courted quiet for years
now filling your ears   with anything that will force it away
    silly girl
this is not the way you treat someone who loved you once
even if you are not a fan
of the dread they spend all their time with these days
you cannot chase who someone used to be
must learn to love them in all their newest forms—
     at your mother's hospital bedside while she sleeps
       onstage when the joke doesn't land
         in the fertility clinic waiting room
           at the vigil through the city streets
           your tears in lockstep with the stranger beside you
             & if your old friend ever picked up the phone again
             you would say
             wherever you've been
             was where you needed to be
             & whoever you are now
             welcome back, beloved.

DEVOTED

shivering in the early evening chill
Kayla is wrapped in a towel & two sweatshirts
one of which is mine
when she says something dumb that makes us laugh
& in the light hush that settles after
she says   *please don't remember I said that*
which makes us laugh harder
because of course we will now   & I know
we don't get to pick   what parts of us
stick to the sides of the bowl
but I sure hope it ends up
being the times I felt soft & borrowed
warm enough & comfortable
& here for as long as you need

in the park I watch Reenie ask a kid to play & get turned down
Reenie—the most extroverted four year old I've ever met
who could strike up repartee with a squirrel or a lamppost
who has tucked me into bed at 7pm
to ensure she didn't miss an opportunity
to play with me after she'd gone to bed
after a second kid rejects her offer
she sulks for a while by the slide
until she notices a boy pretending to make pizza
she approaches slow   tries a new tactic
says   *can I help you make pizza?*
stepping into his invisible kitchen & offering to sous chef
& this is also how I have learned to make friends—
eager to join you in whatever world you are building
to offer my hands for kneading & serving
remembering your dietary restrictions
& your favorite tv show
& your mother's cancer
& your bad back
& the parts of you
you would prefer nobody remembered

& whether or not you run cold
& are sure to need another sweatshirt before the night is through

& the mathematicians want me to know
that infinity   isn't a number
it's a direction you can move
not a destination for reaching   but I knew that
that's the blazing asphalt I try to walk across barefoot
brightest sun I squint directly into
& I'm orbiting it again aren't I
how little   time there is
when I say forever   I mean
I stocked the kitchen with your favorite pizza toppings
I mean   what if we just keep moving   in this direction
I will sit in the passenger seat while you point out
every street corner you ever kissed a crush
I will ride along while you pick up your dry cleaning
& walk through a rose garden that is dead for the winter
not dead   patient
I could learn to be patient   if I knew
there would always be a you to love

EPITHALAMION

for the occasion of my dear friends' wedding

Perhaps you've noticed
the way someone yawning
blooms a yawn in your own mouth
as though it were your idea
& not a hand me down,
the way an ocean wave
is not invented out of nothing, but
arrives from somewhere else,
sent from one shoreline of the lopsided planet
to another, so that every ocean
is the same ocean, no matter
what edge of it you are dipping your toes in.
You can stand on a cliff & watch a storm roll towards you,
passed around the globe like wet gossip,
one storm begetting another,
just as my middle school science teacher taught me
that matter cannot be created nor destroyed,
just shifted from one state to the next,
which is comforting on days you miss the dinosaurs
or need to be reminded that many people had to fall in love
with a face at least a little bit like yours
in order for yours to get here.
Maybe God had a good idea one time
& the rest has all been dominoes:
a thunderclap begets a hiccup begets an undertow begets
your certainty that a face was made for you to love it,
but ask the coral reef, who knows we are not good ideas
& definitely not new ones,
more like galactic putty smushed into human form,
who spend so much of our brief time here
losing sight of the storms we came from,
the weather that moves through us,
that we unleash on everyone else.
& who can blame us?
There is no shame in forgetting

that our atoms
once held together some other jellyfish,
when her cheek on your pillow makes your skin
too electric to be called anything but *New*.
When my grandmother was
nearing the end of her time in the body I knew her in,
she started to lose herself
memory first, but language close behind.
She misused words, mixed up phrases, said things incorrectly.
When she met someone,
instead of saying, *it is a pleasure to meet you,*
she would say,
it is a pleasure to love you.
She understood
that what feels unknown
is an opportunity for remembering.
In which case, in some future,
when two red-shouldered hawks
see each other for what they think is the first time,
they might suddenly recall
that there was once a day
when we traveled many miles,
some of us whole lifetimes,
so that we could meet you,
here, in love,
& what more evidence will they need
(what more evidence do you need?) to see
that it is
a sincere pleasure to love you
again & again.

MY GREAT GRANDCHILDREN
FINALLY GET SKEPTICAL

So which one was it?
She can't have been a wandering poet
who never came home
& a homebody who followed the rules.
Either the stories are true,
about the motorcycles & monsoons,
the romance & the rooftops,
or they aren't.
Either she was voted *Most School Spirit*
or *Most Likely to Get Away with Murder,*
but she can't have been both.
She can't have been blush-plagued &
spotlight-addicted, can't have been
toddler-naive & second-life wise,
she can't have been vulnerability evangelist
& lugged around a padlocked heart,
I have seen the photos.
She was almost six feet tall.
She had piano-fingers & giraffe legs,
how can you tell me she had no grace?
Surely, she must have been able to knot
those limbs into some kind of sex appeal.
She was more dandelion than tulip?
More sudden downpour than summer breeze?
I don't believe you that she never stopped moving.
I mean, everybody stops moving eventually.
Even the earth is slowing down,
& from what I've heard, she was never anybody's planet.
Star, maybe, depending on who you asked,
but also black hole. Also couldn't stop
revolving around herself.
Why does she look the same in every photo?
Like her face never changed?
Like all those train rides & heartbreaks
didn't leave a wrinkle? A grey hair?

Makes it hard to believe.
The ticket stubs
are some kind of evidence, I guess.
Sure, all those notebooks full of scribbles,
but anyone can write a poem.
Anyone can claim an adventure that isn't theirs.
Give me enough time & I bet
I could come up with a pretty good story too.

READER, DEAR

maybe where you are it is nighttime or maybe it is day
maybe someone is reading this to you the way
any dear one of mine would warn you
that going into a bookstore with me entails being read to
like the poetry section is the dressing room I've parked myself outside of
where I keep making you try on poems until we find one that's a good fit
or maybe you're reading to yourself unaccompanied
maybe out loud or maybe in silence
maybe in a special accent you have for poetry that nobody else can hear
maybe you haven't committed yet
maybe you are skimming through pages & trying to decide
whether you can justify *another* book especially one without a twist-ending
maybe you are looking for a gift for someone & you heard somewhere
a book of poems is a good offering   one time
someone broke into my rental car & opened a box of my books
& took the books out but left them all behind & sometimes
I imagine they stopped mid-burglary & flipped through a couple poems
before deciding *mm not for me* so maybe that's what's going on right now
maybe you have broken into my rental car
& are standing there thinking *not again!*   maybe you're heartbroken
& you're looking for someone else to find language
for what doesn't feel languageable   baby I've been there
maybe you've borrowed this   maybe somebody lent it to you
maybe the library or a friend   maybe you stole it
maybe on purpose or maybe the way I borrowed Jeff McDaniel's poetry book
from the Urban Word Library once when I was fourteen & just forgot
& never gave it back because sometimes that is also how burglary works—
so slow & ordinary & unnoticed by even you who are doing the stealing!
& then boom! years have gone by & you're holding something that isn't yours
& somewhere there's a hole that you caused in the fabric of everything
maybe you're sorry   maybe you're guilty
maybe you're as disenchanted as I am by the kingdom of ownership
& are ready to disavow it entirely
to embark somewhere the entire premise is absurd   the only rule
my parents had when I was growing up was   *we share in this family*
which they used to scold me if I was withholding something my brother wanted

but somewhere along the way it morphed into a guideline—*if I have something*
then I have something to share   & that's it I guess: half my sandwich
& also my couch   also my afternoon
also what happened   what I've learned   what makes me laugh
what made me think of you   what I think the poem means
the metaphors I'm using to explain things to myself   what I can't figure out
what I don't want people to know about me &
what I don't want to know about me
& it isn't a superpower it isn't a curse it isn't a legacy it isn't a trap
it is what it is & it is what I've got & you can't steal it
because right about now   is when it becomes yours too

MILES FROM ANY SHORELINE

I frequently miss entire days
caught in my brain's spiderwebs
but if I happen to look up in time
to notice that the darkness
still has a little daylight left to swallow
I will ivy up the fire escape to catch
whatever embers of the day
are still slow-dying behind New Jersey
& last week through the fog
of my loneliness I realized
the living room was slippery pink
which I knew meant
a lightshow must be on display
so with a quickness I reserve for emergencies
I scampered to the roof & sure enough—
an explosion of upside-down clementine
cotton candy cloud wisps
was tie-dyeing the Hudson River neon
& I swear I am not a lightweight
but I was colordrunk immediately
dizzy with gasp & skyward reaching
hoping my fingers might find a bell
I could ring that would summon
all of New York City to look up!
& west! but there was no bell
& nobody to call
just my own astonishment
still willing to answer after the first ring
how predictable: one good sunset
& I release my nihilism
like rose petals behind a bridal gown   look—
I have married my cynicism
& renewed my vows
but it didn't stop the streetlights
from coming on at the exact moment I passed beneath them
when nobody else was in the park to see it
like the whole city was winking

& yes I blushed
the way I do whenever someone beautiful flirts with me
I haven't stopped thinking about death
I am just wringing every last jaw-drop
from the tissue between heartbreaks
on a long run outside the city
along a highway &
miles from any shoreline
I found a starfish   alone on the asphalt
an unsolvable mystery!
with no witness to corroborate
& there I was again
wandering the streets of
Bewilderville: Population 1
what else could I possibly do
but swing wide the doors of my delight
to this patron saint of unbelonging—
fragile & whole & so far from home
if you too have been the one
nobody asked to dance
I have a starfish I'd love to introduce you to
& I don't have any proof
but one time the wind
or my ancestors or unseasonal warmth
carried three hawks to my
kitchen windowsill
to rattle my coffin to cocoon
& two of them left but
one of them stayed
eyed me through the glass like a promise
or a dare
so lately
I am trying
to pick up when the universe calls

NOTES

An earlier version of "Ars Poetica" was published in *We the Gathered Heat,* an anthology of Asian American & Pacific Islander poetry, performance & spoken word, edited by Franny Choi, Bao Phi, No'u Revilla & Terisa Siagatonu for Haymarket Books in September 2024.

"Jakarta, January" was written after Hanif Abdurraqib's poem USAvCuba, which is after Frank O'Hara's poem "The Day Lady Died." An earlier version of "Jakarta, January" was published by the Academy of American Poets' *Poem-a-Day* series in February 2019, selected by Clint Smith. I would like to express gratitude for the students & faculty of the Jakarta Intercultural School, where I was teaching during the events described in this poem, & also to the many people who still came out to see us perform, days after the violence. Additional gratitude to the person who left this comment online under a video of me performing this poem (I generally do not read video comments, but I'm grateful to have had my attention called to this one): "I know the father who walked into Starbucks that morning & had shrapnel pulled from his body the next day. I saw him minutes before he walked out. I still remember hearing the bombs & the gunshots, the smoke in the blue sky. I remember the lockdown, the desperate phone calls. We were adults, huddled together in the safety of a tiny room, but we were nothing more than terrified children in the face of terror. Sarah performed in my hometown, Jakarta, the weekend after the incident. I missed her performance because I was too shaken after the incident to travel anywhere. But that's okay because I still get to hear this incredible poem, one that has come close to my heart. While some people sadly passed away during the incident, you'll be pleased to hear that the father I know survived & has, from I last heard, [sic] become determined to cherish his family & spend more time with them."

"The Places We Are Not" was written while in residence at Vermont Studio Center. An earlier version of this poem was published in BuzzFeed Reader in June 2018, selected by Angel Nafis.

"Dreaming Boy" was written while in residence at Serenbe. An earlier version of this poem was published in the *Catamaran Literary Reader* in October 2015.

Earlier versions of "Table Games," "Hitting Rocks into Useless Bay," & "An Address I'll Forget" were written while in residence at Hedgebrook.

"Orange" references a verse in Sanskrit, which was sent to me as follows:

भवन्ति नम्रास्तरवः फलोद्गमैः
नवाम्बुभिर्भूरिविलिम्बिनो घनाः ।
अनुद्धताः सत्पुरुषाः समृद्धभिः
स्वभाव एवैषः परोपकारिणाम् ॥

An earlier version of "Unreliable" was published in Issue 40 of the *Adroit Journal* in May 2021.

The satirical magazine *Reductress* has a headline that makes me laugh, which is: "REPORT: There's No 'Right' Way to Be Single, but What You're Doing Isn't Great," which I allude to in "Kuchisabishii."

The epigraph for "The Minister of Loneliness" is based on a *Business Insider* headline from December 2020. Statistics on national suicide rates were collected from the Japanese National Police Agency & statistics on COVID-19 deaths were collected from the Japanese Ministry of Health, Labor, & Welfare.

"Devoted" rephrases a quote from Karim Ani on a *Radiolab* episode called "Zeroworld." The complete quote is: "Infinity in mathematics isn't actually a number, it's a direction. It's a direction that we can move towards, but it isn't a destination that we can get to."

If you would like to read "Epithalamion" at a wedding, I recommend changing "red-shouldered hawks" into animals that are meaningful to the people getting married. Making the poem fit them better in this way is not only permitted, but encouraged. Also, I am pretty sure I did not come up with the general concept of "people fell in love with a face like yours in order for yours to get here," but for the life of me I can't figure out where my brain picked it up.

ACKNOWLEDGMENTS

Thank you to Maya Millett, without whom I could not & would not have made this collection & the entire team at The Dial Press & Penguin Random House for their hard work on this book's behalf.

Thank you to Yfat Reiss Gendell, for being in my corner & for seeing another poetry collection on the horizon before I did.

Thank you to the publications where earlier versions of these poems appeared, & the curators & editors who selected them.

Thank you to the places that have given me time & residence with which to work on these poems: Grace Cathedral, Hedgebrook, Kundiman, Serenbe Artists in Residence, & Vermont Studio Center.

Thank you to the entities that have given many of these poems a life beyond the individual stages I shared them on: TED, Button Poetry, & my father's YouTube channel *speakeasynyc,* which he originally created to share poems with me when I went away to college & he wanted to keep me up-to-date on all the poetry I was missing back home. It was born out of an impulse of such generous care & I love that it has grown into something that is enjoyed by so many others too.

Thank you to the many poets who provided doorways through which I could (& needed to) walk, in order to find these poems of my own: Hanif Abdurraqib, Charlotte Abotsi, Elizabeth Acevedo, Kaveh Akbar, Cristin O'Keefe Aptowicz, Fatimah Asghar, Derrick Brown, Laura Lamb Brown-Lavoie, Mahogany L. Browne, Franny Choi, Noah Arhm Choi, Safia Elhillo, Shira Erlichman, Eve L. Ewing, Adam Falkner, Ross Gay, Andrea Gibson, Aracelis Girmay, Omar Holmon, Nancy Kangas, Phil Kaye, Emily King, Paige Lewis, Ada Limón, Rachel McKibbens, Anis Mojgani, Angel Nafis, Hieu Minh Nguyen, Naomi Shihab Nye, Frank O'Hara, Mary Oliver, Jon Sands, Sam Sax, Clint Smith, Danez Smith, Layli Long Soldier, Jeanann Verlee, Jamila Woods, & too many others to list. Your fingerprints are all over these poems, thank you for showing me what is possible.

Thank you to Sophia Janowitz, who has provided the most beautiful drawings for every book project I've ever attempted, & who has provided unwavering companionship for nearly the entirety of our lives. (Mercifully, we had to spend only three months lost & alone before we met, after which we eventually [quite literally] learned to speak, together & to each other, & have been having one continual conversation & collaboration ever since.)

Thank you to the Emotional Historians workshop & community, & Jon Sands specifically, for creating & maintaining such a supportive, generative space in which so many of these poems were first drafted; who provided a utopian island during a pandemic & beyond, without whom half of this book would not exist, or else would have taken me another decade at least.

Thank you to my beloveds, who know who they are.

To my parents—how outrageous to have started life with winning the cosmic lottery on you two.

To my brother—thank you, sorry, thank you, best & most.

Thank you to the surely hundreds, possibly thousands of people who all had a hand in my ability to work as a traveling poet for ten years: Phil Kaye, who dreamed & worked at my side, educators who believed in us &/or poetry enough to invite us into their schools, found siblings & mentors, event organizers & volunteers, patient & generous friends, & everyone who ever came out to see me share poetry live in person.

& thank you to anyone who has reached for a poem of mine, in any medium. That you would spend some of your brief time here with me & my words is an honor that rattles me daily.

ABOUT THE AUTHOR

Sarah Kay is a writer, performer, & educator from New York City. She is the author of four other books of poetry: *B, No Matter the Wreckage, The Type, & All Our Wild Wonder*. Kay is the founder & co-director of Project VOICE, an organization that uses poetry to entertain, educate, & empower students & educators in classrooms & communities worldwide.